INCLUSIVE LEADERSHIP IN THE ARTS

EMBRACING DIVERSITY, EQUITY, AND INCLUSION

DENISE ZUBIZARRETA

© Denise Zubizarreta

Denise Zubizarreta
LEAP Institute for the Arts
Arts Leadership & Cultural Management
Colorado State University

For Mom.

TABLE OF CONTENTS

Prologue — 7

Chapter 1 — 8
The Case for Inclusion in the Arts — 8
Diversity Fuels Creativity — 8
Equity Ensures Fairness and Justice — 9
Inclusion Creates Belonging — 10
Why DEI is a Strategic Imperative — 11

Chapter 2 — 13
Understanding Inclusive Leadership — 13
Key Traits of Inclusive Leaders — 14
Self-Awareness — 14
Empathy — 14
Courage — 15
Curiosity — 15
Practical Tools for Inclusive Leadership — 16
Inclusive Decision-Making — 16
Active Listening Workshops — 16
Bias Interruption Techniques — 17
Additional Strategies for Fostering Inclusive Leadership — 17

Mentorship and Sponsorship Programs	17
Regular Feedback and Reflection	18
Cultural Competence Training	18
Leading with Inclusion	19

Chapter 3   20
Building Inclusive Policies   20

Why Inclusive Policies Matter	20
Steps to Develop Inclusive Policies	21
The Power of Inclusive Policies	26

Chapter 4   27
Designing Inclusive Programs and Practices   27

Strategies for Inclusive Programming	27
Practical Tools for Inclusive Programming	31
Fostering Inclusion Through Programming	37

Chapter 5   38
Embracing Neurodiversity in the Arts   38

Understanding Neurodiversity in the Arts	39
Practical Tools for Supporting Neurodiverse Staff and Audiences	42
Embracing Neurodiversity as a Strength	44

Chapter 6   46
Fostering Cultural Competence   46

Why Cultural Competence Matters in the Arts   46

Strategies to Build Cultural Competence   47

Practical Tools for Building Cultural Competence   51

Leading with Cultural Competence   53

Chapter 7   54

Measuring Impact and Making Continuous Improvements   54

Tools for Measuring DEI Impact   54

Creating a Culture of Continuous Improvement   58

Leading with Inclusion   59

About the Author   61

PROLOGUE

Welcome to Inclusive Leadership in the Arts: Embracing Diversity, Equity, and Inclusion. As a leader in the arts, you already know that creativity thrives on diverse perspectives. The arts should reflect the full spectrum of human experience, yet many organizations still struggle to create truly inclusive environments.

This book is a guide to navigating the complexities of diversity, equity, and inclusion (DEI) in arts organizations. It's about more than just checking boxes—it's about fostering spaces where every voice is heard, every story is valued, and every person feels they belong. Whether you're an executive director, a curator, an educator, or simply passionate about the arts, you'll find practical strategies here to help you build a culture that embraces diversity across race, ethnicity, gender, neurodiversity, and cultural differences.

We'll explore the principles of inclusive leadership, share tools and frameworks for implementing inclusive practices, and offer real-world examples from arts organizations that are getting it right. So, let's dive in and start this journey towards a more inclusive, vibrant arts community.

CHAPTER 1

THE CASE FOR INCLUSION IN THE ARTS

Art is a powerful, universal language that has the unique ability to connect people across different cultures, histories, and experiences. It serves as a medium for expression, dialogue, and transformation. Yet, despite this inherent universality, many arts organizations struggle to reflect the rich diversity of the communities they serve. Leadership and organizational cultures within the arts can often fall short in embracing the full spectrum of human experience, limiting their impact and relevance.

To truly fulfill their mission, arts organizations must move beyond seeing diversity, equity, and inclusion (DEI) as mere buzzwords or checkboxes. Instead, DEI must become a core principle woven into every aspect of their work. Here's why:

Diversity Fuels Creativity

Creativity thrives on diversity. When we bring together people from different backgrounds—racial, ethnic, cultural, socioeconomic, gender, or neurodiverse—we create a fertile ground for innovation and new ideas. Every person brings their unique perspective, informed by their personal experiences and cultural context. This diversity of thought enriches artistic expression, resulting in more dynamic, relevant, and meaningful work that resonates with a broader audience.

In a room filled with diverse voices, ideas are challenged, assumptions are questioned, and new approaches are discovered. This process of dialogue and exchange is essential for artistic innovation. It prevents the stagnation that can occur when organizations rely on homogenous thinking or repeat familiar patterns. When arts organizations commit to diversity, they embrace a wealth of perspectives that push boundaries, inspire new art forms, and keep their work vibrant and evolving.

For example, a theater company that casts actors of various ethnicities in roles traditionally limited to specific demographics brings fresh interpretations and nuances to classic plays. A museum that includes curators and artists from diverse backgrounds can offer exhibits that tell stories from multiple viewpoints, thereby engaging new audiences and sparking broader conversations. Diversity in leadership, staff, artists, and programming ensures that the organization remains relevant and reflective of the world in which it exists.

Equity Ensures Fairness and Justice

Equity goes beyond equality—it recognizes that different people have different needs and that a one-size-fits-all approach is insufficient. While equality focuses on providing everyone with the same resources, equity takes into account the varying challenges and barriers individuals face and ensures they have the support and opportunities they need to succeed.

In the context of arts organizations, equity is about creating fair pathways for all artists, staff, and audiences. This might mean implementing policies and practices that actively remove barriers to participation for underrepresented groups. It could involve providing scholarships for young artists from low-income backgrounds, offering professional development opportunities to staff who face systemic challenges, or developing programs that reach communities that have historically been excluded from mainstream art spaces.

Equity is essential because it addresses the systemic inequities that have long marginalized certain voices in the arts. By focusing on justice—ensuring that all individuals have a fair chance to contribute and thrive—arts organizations can help to level the playing field. When organizations commit to equity, they not only support their current community but also open doors to new talent and audiences who might otherwise be overlooked or ignored. This commitment to fairness and justice strengthens the organization's social impact, reinforces its mission, and enhances its relevance in a diverse society.

Inclusion Creates Belonging

Diversity and equity are critical, but they are not enough without inclusion. Inclusion is about creating a culture where every individual feels valued, respected, and welcomed. It's ensuring that everyone, regardless of their background, identity, or experiences, feels they have a place at the table.

An inclusive environment goes beyond mere representation; it actively seeks out and amplifies underrepresented voices. It means designing processes, spaces, and practices that are welcoming to all, from the way meetings are run to how audiences are engaged. Inclusion involves creating an organizational culture where all members—whether staff, artists, or community participants—feel they can contribute their unique talents and perspectives without fear of discrimination or exclusion.

When people feel included, they are more likely to engage fully, share their ideas, and collaborate effectively. They are also more likely to be committed to the organization's mission, leading to higher morale, stronger team dynamics, and a greater sense of collective purpose. In contrast, when people feel excluded or marginalized, it can lead to disengagement, low productivity, and high turnover—hindering the organization's ability to achieve its goals.

For arts organizations, inclusion translates into a richer, more dynamic creative process. It means offering programs that are accessible to everyone, using inclusive language in marketing and communications, and ensuring that decision-making processes consider a range of perspectives. It also means fostering a workplace culture where all employees, regardless of their background, feel supported and empowered to succeed.

Why DEI is a Strategic Imperative

Ultimately, embracing diversity, equity, and inclusion is not just the right thing to do—it is a strategic imperative for arts organizations. Organizations that are diverse, equitable, and inclusive are better positioned to attract and retain top talent, build strong community partnerships, and engage a wide range of audiences. They are more innovative, resilient, and adaptable in the face of change.

Organizations that prioritize DEI are more likely to receive funding and support from donors, foundations, and public agencies that are increasingly emphasizing these values in their giving criteria. By committing to DEI, arts organizations can strengthen their credibility, enhance their impact, and ensure their long-term sustainability.

To truly fulfill their mission, arts organizations must reflect the rich diversity of the communities they serve. This means moving beyond surface-level commitments and embedding DEI into every aspect of their work—from leadership and governance to programming and audience engagement. Only then can they truly harness the power of the arts to inspire, connect, and transform.

By understanding and implementing DEI principles, arts leaders can foster environments where creativity flourishes, fairness prevails, and everyone feels a genuine sense of belonging. This is the foundation for a vibrant, dynamic, and impactful arts organization in today's world.

CHAPTER 2

UNDERSTANDING INCLUSIVE LEADERSHIP

Inclusive leadership is about more than just making room for diverse voices—it's about actively championing those voices and creating an environment where everyone feels valued, respected, and empowered to contribute. In the arts, where creativity and innovation thrive on diversity of thought, inclusive leadership is essential for cultivating a vibrant organizational culture that reflects the richness of the communities we serve.

Inclusive leaders understand that they don't need to have all the answers; rather, their role is to create a culture where everyone's input is welcomed and where underrepresented voices are actively sought out and uplifted. This approach helps to break down traditional hierarchies and power dynamics, encouraging a collaborative environment where new ideas can flourish, and creative risks can be taken.

But what does it actually mean to be an inclusive leader in the arts? Let's break down some of the key traits that define inclusive leadership and explore practical tools that arts leaders can use to foster inclusivity in their organizations.

Key Traits of Inclusive Leaders

Self-Awareness

The first step toward inclusive leadership is self-awareness—recognizing one's own biases and understanding how they impact decisions and behaviors. Every leader has biases, whether conscious or unconscious, shaped by their personal experiences, cultural background, and societal conditioning. Inclusive leaders actively work to identify these biases and counteract them, ensuring that they do not influence their actions or decisions. This self-reflection might involve seeking feedback from colleagues, engaging in bias training, or using tools like implicit association tests to uncover hidden biases. By being aware of their own limitations, inclusive leaders can make more equitable decisions and create an environment where all voices are heard.

Empathy

Empathy is the ability to understand and share the feelings of others. For inclusive leaders, empathy means going beyond surface-level interactions and truly valuing the diverse experiences and perspectives of those around them. This involves listening deeply, acknowledging others' emotions and challenges, and showing compassion and understanding. In the arts, empathy allows leaders to connect with artists, staff, and audiences in meaningful ways, fostering a sense of community and trust. It encourages leaders to consider the unique needs and experiences of different individuals and to create inclusive environments where everyone feels respected and supported.

Courage

Being an inclusive leader requires courage—the courage to challenge the status quo, speak out against inequity, and take risks in the pursuit of fairness and justice. This may involve calling out discriminatory behavior, advocating for underrepresented voices, or making bold decisions that prioritize diversity and inclusion, even when they are unpopular or face resistance. Courageous leaders are not afraid to confront difficult issues or navigate discomfort. Instead, they view these challenges as opportunities for growth and change. They understand that fostering an inclusive environment requires both vulnerability and strength.

Curiosity

Inclusive leaders possess a strong sense of curiosity—a willingness to learn, ask questions, and embrace discomfort as a catalyst for growth. They are open to new ideas and perspectives, actively seeking out opportunities to expand their understanding of different cultures, experiences, and viewpoints. This curiosity drives them to engage in continuous learning, whether through formal training, reading, or conversations with others. Inclusive leaders recognize that they don't know everything and are eager to learn from those around them. They create a culture of openness and inquiry, where everyone feels encouraged to share their unique perspectives and contribute to the organization's growth.

Practical Tools for Inclusive Leadership

Implementing inclusive leadership practices requires more than just good intentions—it involves concrete actions and strategies that foster a culture of inclusivity. Here are some practical tools and techniques that arts leaders can use to promote diversity, equity, and inclusion in their organizations:

Inclusive Decision-Making

Inclusive leaders ensure that decision-making processes are transparent, participatory, and representative of diverse voices. This involves creating committees or working groups that reflect the diversity of the community and actively involving them in key decisions. By bringing together people with different backgrounds, experiences, and perspectives, leaders can make more informed and equitable decisions that benefit the entire organization. For example, when planning a new exhibition or program, an inclusive leader might convene a diverse advisory board to provide input on content, curation, marketing, and community engagement. This not only ensures that the final product is inclusive but also fosters a sense of ownership and commitment among all stakeholders.

Active Listening Workshops

Active listening is a critical skill for inclusive leadership. It involves fully concentrating on what others are saying, understanding their message, and responding thoughtfully without judgment. Inclusive leaders can develop active listening skills through workshops and training sessions that focus on techniques such as reflective listening, asking open-ended questions, and providing constructive feedback. These workshops can also help leaders recognize common listening barriers, such as biases, distractions, or preconceived notions, and learn how to overcome them. By promoting active listening, leaders create a culture where everyone feels heard and valued, leading to more effective communication and collaboration.

Bias Interruption Techniques

Bias, whether conscious or unconscious, can significantly impact hiring, programming, audience engagement, and other critical areas of arts organizations. Inclusive leaders can implement bias interruption techniques to identify and address bias at its source. This might involve developing standardized hiring practices that minimize bias, such as using structured interviews, diverse hiring panels, and anonymous application processes. In programming, leaders can conduct regular audits to ensure diverse representation in exhibitions, performances, and educational programs. In audience engagement, they can use inclusive language and imagery in marketing materials and actively reach out to underrepresented communities. By proactively interrupting bias, leaders create a more equitable and inclusive environment for all.

Additional Strategies for Fostering Inclusive Leadership

Mentorship and Sponsorship Programs

Inclusive leaders recognize the importance of mentorship and sponsorship in supporting the growth and development of underrepresented individuals within the organization. Mentorship programs provide guidance, support, and advice to emerging leaders, helping them navigate challenges and build their careers. Sponsorship goes a step further by actively advocating for these individuals, opening doors to new opportunities, and promoting their achievements within the organization. By creating structured mentorship and sponsorship programs, inclusive leaders help to build a more diverse pipeline of future leaders and foster a culture of inclusion and support.

Regular Feedback and Reflection

Inclusive leaders create a culture of continuous feedback and reflection, where everyone feels comfortable sharing their experiences, challenges, and ideas for improvement. This might involve conducting regular surveys, holding town hall meetings, or creating anonymous feedback channels. By actively soliciting input from all staff, artists, and audiences, leaders can identify areas for growth and make data-driven decisions that enhance inclusivity. Regular reflection also allows leaders to assess their own progress, identify any gaps or biases, and make adjustments as needed.

Cultural Competence Training

To lead inclusively, leaders must be culturally competent—able to understand, appreciate, and interact effectively with people from diverse cultural backgrounds. Cultural competence training can help leaders develop the skills and knowledge needed to navigate cultural differences, recognize and challenge stereotypes, and build meaningful relationships with individuals from all walks of life. This training can include workshops, seminars, or experiential learning opportunities that expose leaders to different cultures, histories, and perspectives. By building cultural competence, leaders create a more inclusive and welcoming environment for everyone.

Leading with Inclusion

Inclusive leadership is not a static goal but a dynamic process that requires continuous learning, self-reflection, and action. It is about creating a culture where everyone feels valued, respected, and empowered to contribute. By embracing the traits of self-awareness, empathy, courage, and curiosity, and by implementing practical tools such as inclusive decision-making, active listening workshops, and bias interruption techniques, arts leaders can foster a truly inclusive environment.

Ultimately, inclusive leadership is about recognizing that diversity, equity, and inclusion are not just organizational priorities but fundamental to the arts themselves. It is through inclusive leadership that arts organizations can reflect the richness of the human experience, inspire creativity and innovation, and make a lasting impact on their communities. By committing to inclusivity, arts leaders not only fulfill their mission but also create a more just, equitable, and vibrant world for all.

CHAPTER 3

BUILDING INCLUSIVE POLICIES

Policies form the backbone of any organization. They guide decision-making, shape the work environment, and set the standards for how the organization operates. However, even well-intentioned policies can unintentionally create barriers or exclude certain groups if they are not regularly reviewed and updated through the lens of diversity, equity, and inclusion (DEI).

Inclusive policies are essential for ensuring that every individual—whether a staff member, artist, or audience member—feels welcomed, supported, and valued. This chapter will explore the steps arts organizations can take to audit and revise their policies to create a more inclusive environment.

Why Inclusive Policies Matter

Inclusive policies are crucial for several reasons. They help prevent discrimination, promote equity, and foster a sense of belonging within the organization. When policies are inclusive, they ensure that all individuals have equitable access to opportunities, resources, and support, regardless of their background, identity, or abilities.

Moreover, inclusive policies reflect an organization's commitment to DEI, signaling to staff, artists, audiences, and stakeholders that diversity and inclusion are priorities. This commitment builds trust, strengthens relationships, and enhances the organization's reputation within the community.

However, developing inclusive policies requires more than just good intentions. It involves actively reviewing, revising, and creating policies that align with the organization's DEI goals and values. Here are three critical steps to help arts organizations build inclusive policies.

Steps to Develop Inclusive Policies

Conduct a Policy Audit
The first step in developing inclusive policies is to conduct a comprehensive audit of existing policies. This audit should involve a diverse group of staff and stakeholders to ensure a range of perspectives is considered. The goal is to identify any policies that may unintentionally exclude or disadvantage certain groups.

> Gather a Diverse Team: Form a policy review team that includes individuals from different backgrounds, roles, and experiences within the organization. This team should be representative of the diversity you aim to support—consider including staff from various departments, artists, board members, volunteers, and community partners.
>
> Review Policies Through a DEI Lens: Examine each policy carefully, considering how it might impact

different groups of people. For example, does a policy on dress codes unintentionally discriminate against certain cultural or religious practices? Does a remote work policy consider the needs of employees with disabilities? Are hiring practices designed to attract a diverse pool of candidates?

Gather Feedback: Conduct surveys, focus groups, or one-on-one interviews to gather feedback from staff and stakeholders about their experiences with current policies. Ask questions like: Which policies have you found helpful? Which policies do you find unclear or exclusionary? Are there any policies that make it harder for you to do your job or feel included in the organization?

Identify Gaps and Barriers: Based on the feedback and policy review, identify any gaps or barriers that need to be addressed. This might include policies that are outdated, policies that do not align with current DEI goals, or policies that unintentionally create barriers for certain groups.

Rewrite for Clarity and Inclusion

Once the policy audit is complete, the next step is to rewrite policies to ensure they are clear, inclusive, and aligned with the organization's DEI commitments. Inclusive policies should be easy to understand, legally compliant, and reflective of the organization's values.

Use Plain Language: Rewrite policies in plain, accessible language that is free of jargon, legalese, or technical terms. Policies should be written in a way that everyone, regardless of their background or level of education, can understand. For example, instead of using complex language, use straightforward wording and provide examples to clarify what the policy means in practice.

<u>Ensure Accessibility</u>: Make sure that all policies are accessible to everyone, including those with disabilities. This might involve providing policies in multiple formats (e.g., large print, Braille, audio) or translating them into different languages to meet the needs of diverse staff and community members. Consider digital accessibility as well, ensuring that policies are available in formats that can be accessed by screen readers and other assistive technologies.

<u>Reflect DEI Commitments</u>: Ensure that policies reflect the organization's commitment to DEI. For example, a recruitment policy might explicitly state that the organization welcomes applicants from all backgrounds and will make reasonable accommodations for candidates with disabilities. A performance evaluation policy might include guidelines on how to assess contributions to DEI goals as part of an employee's overall performance.

<u>Provide Flexibility Where Needed</u>: Consider whether certain policies could benefit from flexibility to accommodate diverse needs. For example, instead of a strict 9-to-5 work schedule, a flexible work policy could allow employees to adjust their hours to meet

caregiving responsibilities or other personal needs. Flexibility demonstrates the organization's willingness to adapt and support all staff members equitably.

Implement Accountability Measures
Creating inclusive policies is only the beginning. To ensure that these policies are effective and remain aligned with the organization's DEI goals, it is essential to implement accountability measures.

> Regular Reviews and Updates: Establish a schedule for regularly reviewing and updating policies to ensure they continue to meet the organization's needs and reflect best practices in DEI. This might involve an annual policy review process led by the DEI committee or policy review team. Regular reviews help to identify new barriers or gaps that may emerge over time and allow the organization to respond proactively.
>
> Feedback Mechanisms: Develop systems for gathering ongoing feedback on policies from staff, artists, and stakeholders. This could include anonymous suggestion boxes, regular feedback surveys, or open forums where individuals can voice their concerns or suggestions. Make sure these feedback channels are accessible and safe for everyone, ensuring that no one feels penalized for speaking up.

Tracking and Measuring Impact: Use data to track the impact of policies on the organization's DEI goals. For example, monitor hiring and retention rates to see if new recruitment policies are increasing diversity among staff. Track participation rates in professional development programs to ensure that all employees have equitable access. Use this data to make informed decisions about which policies are working and where adjustments may be needed.

Transparency and Communication: Communicate clearly and transparently about any policy changes, including the rationale behind them and how they support the organization's DEI goals. Use multiple communication channels (e.g., emails, staff meetings, intranet) to ensure that all staff are aware of the changes and understand their implications. Transparency builds trust and helps to create a culture where everyone feels included and informed.

Leadership Accountability: Ensure that leaders and managers are held accountable for implementing and upholding inclusive policies. This might involve including DEI-related goals in their performance evaluations or providing regular training on how to apply inclusive policies in their day-to-day work. Leadership accountability is critical for modeling the behavior and values that the organization aims to promote.

The Power of Inclusive Policies

Building inclusive policies is not just a matter of compliance—it is a powerful tool for creating a more equitable, welcoming, and vibrant organization. By auditing existing policies, rewriting them for clarity and inclusion, and implementing accountability measures, arts organizations can ensure that their policies actively support their DEI goals.

Inclusive policies help to create an environment where all individuals, regardless of their background, feel valued, supported, and empowered to contribute their talents. They demonstrate the organization's commitment to equity and inclusion, helping to attract and retain diverse talent, engage a broader audience, and strengthen community ties.

Ultimately, inclusive policies are about more than just words on paper—they are a reflection of the organization's values and a catalyst for positive change. By committing to inclusivity at every level, arts leaders can create a more just, equitable, and vibrant arts community for all.

CHAPTER 4

DESIGNING INCLUSIVE PROGRAMS AND PRACTICES

Inclusive programming goes beyond just ensuring that a variety of artists are represented on stage or in exhibitions; it's about genuinely engaging with the community in meaningful ways and creating experiences that resonate with diverse audiences. To achieve this, arts organizations need to be intentional about inclusivity from the initial stages of program development to the final delivery and evaluation. Inclusive programs not only foster a sense of belonging and participation but also deepen the organization's impact by making the arts accessible and relevant to everyone.

This chapter explores strategies and practical tools for designing inclusive programs and practices, ensuring that arts organizations can create spaces where all individuals, regardless of background or ability, feel welcomed and valued.

Strategies for Inclusive Programming

Community-Centric Approach
An inclusive arts organization must prioritize a community-centric approach to programming. This means actively

engaging with local communities to understand their needs, interests, and experiences and incorporating these insights into program development. It's about creating programs with the community, rather than for them, ensuring that their voices are heard and reflected in the organization's offerings.

> <u>Collaborate with Community Groups</u>: Building partnerships with local organizations, cultural groups, and community leaders is essential for understanding the unique dynamics of the communities you serve. Regular meetings, listening sessions, and collaborative projects can help organizations develop programs that resonate with the community's needs and experiences. For example, an art museum might work with local cultural organizations to co-curate exhibitions that celebrate the artistic contributions of underrepresented groups or host workshops that address community-specific issues.
>
> <u>Engage in Active Outreach</u>: Go beyond the organization's existing audience to reach those who may feel excluded or underrepresented. This might involve conducting outreach in different neighborhoods, working with local schools or community centers, or partnering with organizations that serve marginalized groups. For example, a theater could collaborate with community centers in underserved areas to offer free acting classes or discounted tickets, thus creating a bridge between the organization and new audiences.

Reflect Community Stories and Experiences: Ensure that programming reflects the lived experiences of the community. This could involve commissioning works by local artists, hosting discussions on local issues, or creating programs that explore the community's history, culture, and social dynamics. When people see their stories reflected in the arts, it fosters a sense of ownership, belonging, and engagement.

Accessible Art Spaces

True inclusivity in programming means ensuring that everyone, regardless of ability, can fully participate in and enjoy the organization's offerings. This requires creating physically and sensory-accessible spaces that accommodate a wide range of needs.

Physical Accessibility: Evaluate your facilities to ensure they are fully accessible to people with disabilities. This includes installing ramps, elevators, and accessible bathrooms, providing designated seating for people with mobility challenges, and ensuring that entrances, exits, and pathways are clear and easy to navigate. Additionally, signage should be clear and readable, with tactile or braille options where possible.

Sensory-Friendly Options: Consider the sensory needs of diverse audiences, including those who are neurodiverse or have sensory processing differences. Offer sensory-friendly performances or events with reduced noise, lighting adjustments, and quiet areas for people who may need a break. For example, a theater might offer a "relaxed performance" with adjusted lighting and sound levels, allowing attendees to move freely or make noise without fear of judgment.

Multiple Engagement Formats: Provide different ways for people to engage with art that accommodates various learning and participation styles. This could include offering tactile tours for visually impaired visitors, providing written descriptions or audio guides, and ensuring that virtual content is captioned and screen-reader accessible. For example, a gallery could offer virtual tours for those who cannot attend in person or provide accessible digital programs.

Diverse Representation
Representation matters in the arts. It's essential to commit to showcasing a diverse range of artists, performers, speakers, and curators from various backgrounds to reflect the richness of human experience.

Intentional Diversity: Be deliberate in ensuring that diversity is reflected across all aspects of programming—from the artists whose work is exhibited or performed to the curators, guest speakers, and workshop facilitators involved. Set concrete goals for representation and establish partnerships with artists and cultural practitioners from underrepresented groups. For instance, a gallery might create an annual exhibition specifically for emerging artists from marginalized communities, or a theater company might prioritize producing plays by women, LGBTQ+, or BIPOC playwrights.

Avoid Tokenism: Authentic diversity goes beyond mere token representation. Ensure that the inclusion of diverse voices is meaningful and integrated throughout the organization's programming, rather than a one-off or checkbox exercise. Avoid presenting works by diverse artists only during specific months or events; instead, incorporate them into the regular program schedule. For example, rather than only featuring Indigenous artists during Indigenous Peoples' Month, strive to include their work throughout the year as an integral part of the organization's programming.

Engage Diverse Audiences: Work to reach a broader audience by creating programs that appeal to a wide range of cultural and social groups. Use inclusive marketing strategies, such as multilingual materials or targeted outreach campaigns, to ensure that all audiences feel welcome and represented. Hosting culturally-specific events or festivals can also help attract new audiences and foster cross-cultural dialogue.

Practical Tools for Inclusive Programming

Program Co-Design
One of the most effective ways to ensure that programs are inclusive is to engage community members in the design and planning process. Co-design involves collaborating with a

diverse group of stakeholders, including artists, community members, and representatives from local organizations, to develop programs that reflect their needs and interests.

> Community Advisory Boards: Establish advisory boards made up of community members from different backgrounds to provide input and guidance on programming decisions. These boards can help identify community needs, suggest relevant themes or topics, and provide feedback on proposed programs. This approach ensures that programming is aligned with community values and priorities.

> Collaborative Workshops: Host workshops or brainstorming sessions with community members to co-create program ideas. Encourage open dialogue and actively seek input from a wide range of voices. For example, a museum might hold a series of workshops with local artists, educators, and community leaders to co-create an exhibition that reflects the community's history and culture.

Accessibility Audits
Regular accessibility audits are essential for ensuring that all aspects of an organization's facilities and practices are welcoming and accessible to everyone.

> Physical Accessibility Assessments: Conduct regular assessments of the organization's physical spaces to identify any barriers to accessibility. This might include evaluating entrances and exits, seating arrangements, signage, restrooms, and parking.

Partner with accessibility consultants or disability advocacy organizations to ensure that assessments are thorough and that recommendations reflect best practices.

- Entrances and Exits: Ensure that all entry and exit points are accessible, with ramps or elevators for people with mobility impairments and automatic doors or push-button access.

- Seating Arrangements: Offer flexible seating options that can accommodate various needs, such as spaces for wheelchairs, wider aisles, and ergonomic seating.

- Signage: Provide clear and readable signage, with braille or tactile options and high-contrast colors to assist those with visual impairments.

- Restrooms: Ensure accessible restrooms are available with proper support features, such as grab bars and lower sinks and dispensers.

- Parking: Designate accessible parking spots close to entrances and ensure they are clearly marked.

   Digital Accessibility Reviews: Ensure that all digital content, including websites, social media, and virtual programming, is accessible to people with disabilities. This includes providing captioning for videos, using alt text for images, ensuring compatibility with screen readers, and providing content in multiple formats (e.g., text, audio, visual).

Regularly review digital platforms and update them to comply with accessibility standards.

- Video Content: Provide closed captions and transcripts for all video content.

- Website Accessibility: Ensure the website is navigable by keyboard, compatible with screen readers, and has adjustable font sizes and contrast settings.

- Alternative Formats: Offer content in multiple formats to cater to different needs, including downloadable documents that are accessible.

<u>Neurodiverse Needs in Spaces</u>: Neurodiversity recognizes that neurological differences—such as autism, ADHD, dyslexia, and sensory processing disorders—are natural variations of the human experience. To make spaces more inclusive for neurodiverse individuals, organizations should consider:

- Sensory-Friendly Spaces: Create sensory-friendly spaces that offer a calm, quiet environment for those who may be overwhelmed by noise or crowds. This could include designated quiet rooms or areas with dim lighting, noise-canceling headphones, and comfortable seating.

- Adjustable Lighting and Sound: Use adjustable lighting and sound levels in spaces to accommodate different sensory needs. Dimmable lights, natural lighting options, and the ability to adjust sound levels can help create a more comfortable environment for neurodiverse individuals.

Ensure that any sudden or flashing lights are minimized or clearly marked.

- Clear Signage and Wayfinding: Provide clear, straightforward signage and wayfinding that uses visual symbols or simple language to assist those who may find complex instructions challenging. Color-coded maps or simple icons can help neurodiverse visitors navigate spaces more easily.

- Flexible Seating Arrangements: Offer flexible seating options, such as allowing individuals to choose where they sit or providing options that enable movement (e.g., rocking chairs or standing desks). This can help accommodate the needs of those who find it difficult to remain seated or still for extended periods.

- Structured and Predictable Schedules: Communicate clear, structured, and predictable schedules for events, performances, or exhibitions. Provide detailed information about what attendees can expect, including any sensory experiences (like loud sounds or flashing lights), to help neurodiverse individuals prepare in advance.

- Sensory-Friendly Programs: Develop sensory-friendly programs, performances, or events specifically designed to cater to neurodiverse audiences. These might include relaxed performances with adjusted lighting and sound, opportunities for audience members to move freely, and spaces where attendees can retreat if they need a break.

- Training for Staff and Volunteers: Train staff and volunteers to recognize and understand the needs of neurodiverse individuals, including how to communicate effectively and respectfully. Provide guidance on offering support, such as providing quiet areas, adjusting lighting, or offering alternative forms of engagement.

Audience Feedback Loops

Creating channels for ongoing audience feedback is critical for understanding the impact of programs and identifying areas for improvement. Feedback loops allow organizations to continuously refine and enhance their offerings based on the needs and preferences of diverse audiences.

Surveys and Feedback Forms: Provide multiple ways for audiences to share their experiences and feedback, such as through surveys, feedback forms, or digital comment platforms. Ensure that feedback tools are accessible and available in multiple languages to reach a broader audience.

Focus Groups and Listening Sessions: Host focus groups or listening sessions with different audience segments to gather deeper insights into their experiences and expectations. Encourage open dialogue and create a safe space where participants feel comfortable sharing their honest opinions.

Responsive Programming Adjustments: Use the feedback gathered to make data-driven adjustments to programming. For example, if feedback indicates that certain groups feel excluded from a program, consider modifying the format, content, or delivery to be more inclusive. Communicate any changes to audiences to show that their input is valued and that the organization is committed to continuous improvement.

Fostering Inclusion Through Programming

Designing inclusive programs and practices is about more than just filling a quota or meeting a checklist—it's about creating genuine connections with diverse communities and ensuring that everyone feels welcomed, respected, and represented in the arts. By adopting a community-centric approach, ensuring accessible art spaces, and committing to diverse representation, arts organizations can develop programs that resonate with a broad audience and foster a sense of belonging.

Practical tools such as program co-design, accessibility audits, and audience feedback loops provide the foundation for this work, enabling organizations to continuously adapt and improve their offerings. Ultimately, inclusive programming strengthens the organization's mission, enhances its impact, and contributes to a more equitable, dynamic, and vibrant arts community.

CHAPTER 5

EMBRACING NEURODIVERSITY IN THE ARTS

Neurodiversity—the understanding that neurological differences such as autism, ADHD, dyslexia, and other cognitive variations are natural and valuable forms of human diversity—represents a critical yet often overlooked dimension of inclusivity in the arts. Neurodiverse individuals bring unique perspectives, skills, and ways of thinking that can enhance creativity, innovation, and problem-solving in arts organizations. However, traditional work environments and programming practices are not always designed to accommodate these differences, which can inadvertently exclude or disadvantage neurodiverse people.

This chapter explores how arts organizations can create inclusive environments that welcome neurodiverse individuals, both as staff and audience members. By rethinking traditional roles, creating flexible workspaces, and tailoring communication styles, arts organizations can build a culture that values and leverages the strengths of neurodiverse individuals, while also providing practical tools to support their inclusion.

Understanding Neurodiversity in the Arts

Rethink Traditional Roles

Many neurodiverse individuals possess unique strengths that can greatly benefit arts organizations. For example, individuals with autism might have exceptional attention to detail, pattern recognition, and memory skills. Those with ADHD often excel in creative problem-solving, thinking outside the box, and working in dynamic environments. People with dyslexia may bring strong visual-spatial skills, innovative thinking, and a unique perspective on narrative and storytelling.

To harness these strengths, arts organizations should rethink traditional roles and job descriptions to be more flexible and inclusive of diverse skills and working styles. This might involve creating roles that are tailored to specific strengths, such as data analysis, visual arts, or creative strategy. It could also mean offering job-sharing opportunities or roles that allow for non-linear thinking and creative experimentation.

> <u>Leveraging Unique Strengths</u>: Redefine roles to focus on specific strengths that neurodiverse individuals bring to the organization. For example, an individual with strong pattern recognition skills could excel in curatorial roles or roles that involve cataloging and organizing large amounts of information. Similarly, someone with a knack for creative problem-solving might thrive in roles related to community engagement or audience development, where innovative thinking is key.

>Flexible Role Descriptions: Move away from rigid job descriptions that focus solely on conventional qualifications or specific experience and instead emphasize the skills, talents, and unique contributions that each candidate can bring. Use inclusive language that encourages a wide range of applicants to consider applying, highlighting the organization's commitment to diversity and neurodiversity.

Create Flexible Workspaces

Neurodiverse individuals may have different sensory needs and preferences when it comes to their working environment. For some, bright lights, loud noises, or open-plan office spaces can be overwhelming and distracting. For others, having a quiet, focused environment may be essential for productivity. To create an inclusive workplace, organizations should design spaces that accommodate a range of sensory needs.

> Quiet Areas and Sensory-Friendly Spaces: Designate quiet areas or sensory-friendly spaces within the organization where staff can go to decompress or work in a low-stimulation environment. These spaces might include soundproof rooms, areas with dimmable or natural lighting, or spaces equipped with sensory tools such as noise-canceling headphones or fidget objects.

> Flexible Lighting and Seating Options: Use adjustable lighting options, such as task lighting or dimmable lights, to accommodate different visual preferences.

Offer various seating arrangements, including standing desks, ergonomic chairs, or rocking chairs, to provide neurodiverse staff with choices that support their comfort and concentration.

Sensory Mapping: Conduct sensory mapping of the workplace to identify areas that may be overly stimulating or challenging for neurodiverse staff. Adjust spaces accordingly to reduce sensory overload, such as adding acoustic panels to reduce noise or rearranging furniture to create quieter zones.

Tailor Communication Styles

Neurodiverse individuals often have different communication preferences and needs. Some may prefer written communication to process information at their own pace, while others may benefit from visual aids, diagrams, or verbal explanations. To foster an inclusive environment, it is important to provide multiple modes of communication and adapt communication styles to meet the needs of neurodiverse staff and audiences.

Multi-Modal Communication: Offer a variety of communication methods, including visual (e.g., infographics, diagrams), verbal (e.g., spoken instructions, discussions), and written (e.g., emails, handouts). Encourage team members to share their preferred communication style and provide opportunities for different types of interactions.

> Clear and Concise Language: Use clear and straightforward language in both internal and external communications. Avoid jargon, ambiguous terms, or overly complex phrasing that may be difficult for some individuals to understand. Provide summaries or bullet points to highlight key information.
>
> Visual Schedules and Instructions: Use visual schedules, calendars, or checklists to help neurodiverse individuals plan their work and activities. Provide visual cues or symbols in documents, presentations, and meetings to help convey information more effectively.

Practical Tools for Supporting Neurodiverse Staff and Audiences

To effectively support neurodiverse individuals, arts organizations should implement practical tools and strategies that promote inclusion and accessibility:

> Training Programs: Develop training programs for staff to understand neurodiversity, recognize the strengths and needs of neurodiverse individuals, and learn inclusive communication techniques. Training can cover topics such as identifying and reducing sensory triggers, using clear and direct language, and providing multiple communication channels. Additionally, train staff on neurodiversity-friendly practices, such as respecting different processing times, accommodating sensory needs, and offering flexible work arrangements. This training can help

create a more supportive and understanding workplace culture.

Flexible Policies: Implement flexible workplace policies that accommodate the needs of neurodiverse staff. This could include offering flexible working hours, remote work options, or allowing breaks as needed to manage sensory overload or concentration challenges. Recognize that different individuals have different peak productivity times, and consider allowing flexibility in work schedules to accommodate these differences. Flexible policies should also extend to accommodations in dress codes, communication styles, or workspace preferences.

Sensory-Friendly Events: Offer sensory-friendly performances, exhibitions, or workshops that cater to the needs of neurodiverse audiences. These events might involve adjusting lighting and sound levels, providing a sensory-friendly environment with quiet areas or fidget tools, and allowing attendees to move freely or take breaks as needed. Sensory-friendly events help create a welcoming and accessible experience for neurodiverse individuals, ensuring they can fully participate and enjoy the organization's offerings.

Develop Guidelines for Sensory-Friendly Programming: Create clear guidelines for what constitutes a sensory-friendly event, including information on lighting, sound, space setup, and audience expectations. Use these guidelines to train staff and volunteers on how to create and facilitate these events.

<u>Advertise Sensory-Friendly Offerings</u>: Clearly promote sensory-friendly events in marketing materials, using inclusive language and providing detailed information about what to expect. This helps neurodiverse audiences plan their visit and feel confident about attending.

<u>Gather Feedback from Neurodiverse Audiences</u>: After sensory-friendly events, gather feedback from neurodiverse attendees to learn what worked well and what could be improved. Use this feedback to continuously enhance the inclusivity and accessibility of your programming.

Embracing Neurodiversity as a Strength

Neurodiversity offers a wealth of strengths and perspectives that can enrich arts organizations and enhance their creative output. By rethinking traditional roles, creating flexible workspaces, tailoring communication styles, and implementing practical tools to support neurodiverse individuals, arts leaders can create an environment where everyone feels valued, included, and empowered to contribute their unique talents.

By embracing neurodiversity as an integral part of their DEI efforts, arts organizations not only foster a more inclusive and equitable workplace but also expand their creative horizons, engage new audiences, and build stronger connections with their communities. In doing so, they reflect the true diversity of human experience and make the arts more accessible and relevant to all.

CHAPTER 6

FOSTERING CULTURAL COMPETENCE

Cultural competence is the ability to understand, respect, and effectively interact with people from diverse cultural backgrounds. For arts organizations, cultural competence is more than a skill—it's a fundamental commitment to inclusivity, ensuring that the organization reflects and serves its community's rich diversity. It involves recognizing that different cultural perspectives bring unique insights, creativity, and value to the organization and finding ways to integrate these perspectives into every aspect of its operations.

Building cultural competence requires ongoing effort and a willingness to learn, adapt, and grow. This chapter explores strategies that arts leaders can use to foster cultural competence within their organizations, creating an environment where diverse voices are valued, and cultural differences are celebrated.

Why Cultural Competence Matters in the Arts

Arts organizations are uniquely positioned to serve as cultural ambassadors, fostering understanding, empathy, and dialogue among diverse communities. By developing cultural competence, arts leaders can ensure that their organizations are more inclusive, equitable, and responsive to the needs and interests of their communities.

Cultural competence helps organizations avoid misunderstandings, build trust, and create programming that resonates with a broader audience. It also enhances the organization's credibility and relevance, attracting diverse talent, partners, and supporters. Ultimately, cultural competence is about creating an environment where everyone feels seen, heard, and valued, regardless of their cultural background.

Strategies to Build Cultural Competence

Cultural Awareness Training
Cultural awareness training is an essential strategy for building cultural competence within arts organizations. Regular workshops and training sessions can help staff and leaders understand different cultural norms, values, and practices, fostering empathy and respect for diverse perspectives.

> Understanding Cultural Differences: Cultural awareness training helps staff recognize the nuances of cultural differences, from communication styles and body language to attitudes toward authority, time, and collaboration. For example, in some cultures, direct eye contact is considered a sign of confidence, while in others, it may be seen as disrespectful. By understanding these differences, staff can interact more effectively and sensitively with diverse audiences, artists, and colleagues.

Addressing Unconscious Bias: Training can also help staff identify and address unconscious biases that may affect their interactions with others. Unconscious biases are automatic, often unintentional attitudes or stereotypes that affect decision-making. By becoming aware of these biases, staff can actively work to counteract them and create a more inclusive and equitable environment.

Fostering Inclusive Communication: Workshops can teach inclusive communication techniques, such as active listening, using inclusive language, and avoiding assumptions based on cultural stereotypes. This ensures that all individuals feel respected and valued in their interactions with the organization.

Continuous Learning Opportunities: Cultural awareness training should not be a one-time event but rather a continuous learning process. Organizations can offer regular training sessions, bring in guest speakers from diverse backgrounds, and provide resources such as books, articles, and videos to help staff deepen their cultural knowledge and understanding over time.

Diverse Hiring Practices
To build cultural competence, arts organizations must prioritize diversity in hiring, not just in terms of numbers but also in terms of experiences, perspectives, and backgrounds. A diverse workforce brings a wide range of cultural insights, creative approaches, and lived experiences that can enhance

the organization's ability to connect with diverse communities and audiences.

> Expand Recruitment Channels: Reach out to diverse talent pools by advertising job openings in a variety of platforms, including those specifically focused on underrepresented groups. Partner with community organizations, cultural groups, and educational institutions that serve diverse populations to build a more diverse applicant pool.
>
> Inclusive Job Descriptions: Write job descriptions that use inclusive language and avoid unnecessary requirements that may deter candidates from applying. For example, instead of specifying a degree requirement, focus on the skills and experiences that are truly essential for the role. Emphasize the organization's commitment to diversity, equity, and inclusion to attract candidates who share these values.
>
> Diverse Hiring Panels: Create diverse hiring panels that represent different cultural backgrounds, perspectives, and experiences. This helps to minimize bias in the selection process and ensures that multiple viewpoints are considered when evaluating candidates.
>
> Bias Interruption Techniques: Implement techniques to interrupt bias in hiring, such as using structured interview questions, blind recruitment processes (where identifying information is removed from

applications), and standardized evaluation criteria. These practices help create a fairer and more equitable hiring process.

Retention and Advancement: Beyond hiring, organizations should focus on retaining and advancing diverse talent. This might involve creating mentorship or sponsorship programs, offering professional development opportunities, and ensuring equitable access to leadership positions. A diverse and inclusive workplace fosters a culture where all employees feel valued, supported, and empowered to grow.

Celebrate Cultural Events

Recognizing and celebrating a wide range of cultural events and traditions within the organization is another effective strategy for building cultural competence. Celebrating cultural events creates an inclusive environment where everyone feels that their culture and identity are valued and respected.

Host Cultural Celebrations: Organize events that celebrate cultural holidays, festivals, and traditions from around the world. These events could include performances, exhibitions, workshops, or community gatherings that showcase the art, music, dance, food, and customs of different cultures. For example, an organization might host a Lunar New Year celebration with traditional performances, crafts, and food, or organize an Indigenous Peoples' Day event featuring local Indigenous artists and storytellers.

Acknowledge Diverse Holidays: Make a conscious effort to acknowledge and celebrate diverse holidays, both in internal communications and in public programming. This might involve sharing information about different cultural holidays in newsletters, on social media, or in public announcements, and offering flexible scheduling or time off for employees who observe these holidays.

Inclusive Programming: Incorporate diverse cultural perspectives into regular programming by featuring artists, performers, and speakers from a wide range of backgrounds. For example, a theater could produce plays that explore different cultural narratives, or a museum could curate exhibitions that highlight art from various cultural traditions. This approach ensures that diverse voices are represented year-round, not just during specific cultural events.

Community Partnerships: Collaborate with local cultural organizations, community groups, and cultural leaders to co-create events and programs that reflect the community's diversity. This not only helps build stronger relationships with diverse communities but also ensures that the organization's programming is relevant and meaningful to its audience.

Practical Tools for Building Cultural Competence

To effectively build cultural competence, arts organizations can implement several practical tools and practices:

Cultural Competence Assessments: Conduct regular assessments to evaluate the organization's cultural competence. These assessments might include surveys, focus groups, or self-assessment tools that help staff reflect on their cultural knowledge, attitudes, and practices. Use the findings to identify areas for growth and set goals for improvement.

Diversity and Inclusion Task Forces: Create a task force or committee dedicated to advancing cultural competence within the organization. This group can lead initiatives such as cultural awareness training, diverse hiring practices, and cultural celebrations, ensuring that DEI goals are integrated into all aspects of the organization's operations.

Cultural Ambassadors: Identify and empower cultural ambassadors within the organization who can help foster cultural competence by sharing their knowledge, experiences, and perspectives. These ambassadors might lead workshops, provide mentorship, or serve as a resource for colleagues seeking to learn more about different cultures.

Cross-Cultural Exchanges: Facilitate cross-cultural exchanges by encouraging staff, artists, and audiences to engage with different cultural perspectives. This might involve hosting artist residencies, exchange programs, or international collaborations that bring diverse voices together.

<u>Feedback and Reflection</u>: Create opportunities for ongoing feedback and reflection on cultural competence efforts. Encourage staff and community members to share their experiences, challenges, and suggestions for improvement. Use this feedback to continuously refine and enhance cultural competence initiatives.

Leading with Cultural Competence

Building cultural competence is an ongoing journey that requires commitment, openness, and a willingness to learn. By implementing strategies such as cultural awareness training, diverse hiring practices, and celebrating cultural events, arts leaders can create an environment where all cultures are valued, respected, and represented.

Cultural competence enhances the organization's ability to connect with diverse communities, foster meaningful dialogue, and create art that reflects the full spectrum of human experience. By embracing cultural competence, arts organizations not only fulfill their mission of inclusivity but also build a more vibrant, dynamic, and impactful cultural community.

CHAPTER 7

MEASURING IMPACT AND MAKING CONTINUOUS IMPROVEMENTS

Building an inclusive organization is not a one-time effort but an ongoing process that requires continuous assessment, adaptation, and improvement. As arts leaders, it is crucial to regularly measure your progress in diversity, equity, and inclusion (DEI) to ensure that your initiatives are effective and that your organization is moving in the right direction. Measuring progress allows you to identify successes, pinpoint areas for growth, and make informed decisions about how to adjust and enhance your DEI efforts over time.

This chapter focuses on practical tools for measuring DEI impact and creating a culture of continuous improvement. By using these tools and strategies, arts organizations can ensure they are fostering an environment where everyone feels valued and included, while staying accountable to their DEI goals.

Tools for Measuring DEI Impact

Surveys and Feedback
Regular surveys and feedback are powerful tools for gauging perceptions of inclusivity and identifying areas for

improvement. Surveys can be conducted with staff, artists, audiences, and other stakeholders to gather insights into their experiences and perceptions related to DEI within the organization.

> Anonymous Surveys: Implement anonymous surveys to encourage honest and open feedback without fear of repercussions. Ask questions about participants' sense of belonging, their perception of inclusivity, and any challenges they have faced. Include both quantitative questions (e.g., "On a scale of 1 to 5, how included do you feel in the organization?") and qualitative questions (e.g., "What specific changes would make you feel more included?").
>
> Focus Groups and Listening Sessions: Complement surveys with focus groups and listening sessions that provide a more in-depth understanding of people's experiences and perspectives. These sessions can be organized for different groups (e.g., employees, artists, audiences) to gather detailed feedback and foster open dialogue about DEI issues.
>
> Regularly Review Feedback: Make it a priority to regularly review feedback collected from surveys and listening sessions. Use this information to identify recurring themes, concerns, and areas of improvement. Develop action plans based on this feedback and communicate these plans back to your community to demonstrate that their input is valued and acted upon.

Diversity Metrics

Tracking diversity metrics across all levels of the organization is essential for understanding where you stand and where improvements are needed. These metrics provide a clear picture of representation within the organization and help identify any gaps or areas of inequity.

> Representation Data: Track diversity metrics for various demographic categories, including race, ethnicity, gender, age, disability, socioeconomic background, and more. Monitor representation across different levels of the organization, such as board members, leadership teams, staff, artists, and audiences. For example, collect data on the diversity of applicants, hires, promotions, and retention rates to assess whether equitable practices are in place.
>
> Audience Demographics: Track audience demographics to understand who is attending your programs and events. Use tools such as ticketing data, surveys, and registration forms to collect this information. Analyze the data to determine whether your audiences reflect the diversity of your community and identify any underrepresented groups.
>
> Equity Audits: Conduct regular equity audits to assess how resources, opportunities, and support are distributed within the organization. These audits can reveal patterns of inequity in hiring, compensation, professional development, and access to decision-

making processes, helping you identify areas for targeted improvement.

Benchmarking and Goal-Setting

Setting specific, measurable DEI goals and benchmarking progress against them is critical for driving meaningful change. Goals provide a clear direction for your DEI efforts, while benchmarking allows you to track progress over time and make necessary adjustments.

> SMART Goals: Develop DEI goals that are Specific, Measurable, Achievable, Relevant, and Time-bound (SMART). For example, set a goal to increase the representation of people of color in leadership positions by 20% within two years or to achieve gender parity on your board of directors by a specific date.
>
> Progress Indicators: Identify key performance indicators (KPIs) that align with your DEI goals. These could include metrics such as the number of diverse hires, retention rates for underrepresented groups, participation rates in DEI training, or audience diversity metrics. Regularly track and report on these indicators to assess progress.
>
> Benchmarking Against Peers: Compare your organization's progress against similar arts organizations or industry benchmarks to understand how you measure up and identify best practices. This can provide motivation for continuous improvement and help you stay competitive in the field.

Creating a Culture of Continuous Improvement

To build an inclusive organization, it's essential to foster a culture of continuous improvement where DEI efforts are regularly assessed, celebrated, and refined. Here are practical strategies to cultivate this culture:

> Regular Check-Ins: Schedule regular check-ins to assess DEI progress and make adjustments as needed. These check-ins can be monthly, quarterly, or semi-annual meetings where DEI committees, leadership teams, and staff come together to review progress, share updates, and discuss any challenges or opportunities. Use these sessions to hold the organization accountable, set new goals, and brainstorm innovative strategies to address ongoing challenges.
>
> Celebrate Wins: Recognize and celebrate achievements in DEI, both big and small, to build momentum and morale. Publicly acknowledge progress, such as reaching a diversity milestone, launching a successful inclusive program, or completing a round of cultural competence training. Celebrating these wins reinforces the importance of DEI and motivates staff, artists, and stakeholders to stay committed to the organization's goals.
>
> Stay Flexible: Be open to feedback and willing to adapt strategies as needed. Understand that DEI is not a one-size-fits-all approach and that what works for one organization may not work for another. Stay

responsive to the changing needs of your community, staff, and audiences, and be prepared to adjust your DEI plans based on new information, feedback, or external factors. Flexibility and adaptability are key to ensuring that your DEI efforts remain relevant and effective.

<u>Engage All Stakeholders</u>: Foster a sense of ownership and commitment to DEI by engaging all stakeholders in the process. This includes staff, board members, artists, audiences, and community partners. Encourage everyone to contribute their perspectives, ideas, and feedback to create a shared vision for inclusion. When everyone feels invested in the organization's DEI journey, there is a greater likelihood of sustained momentum and impact.

Leading with Inclusion

Inclusive leadership is not a destination; it's an ongoing journey that requires continuous reflection, learning, and adaptation. It's about being open to growth, willing to make mistakes, and committed to making meaningful changes that reflect your organization's values and mission.

By embracing diversity in all its forms and fostering an environment of equity and inclusion, arts leaders can create vibrant, dynamic organizations that truly reflect and serve their communities. Remember that every small step you take toward inclusion strengthens the foundation of your organization, making it more resilient, creative, and capable of achieving its mission.

As you apply these tools and frameworks, stay mindful of the fact that building an inclusive organization is a collective effort that benefits from the input and engagement of all stakeholders. Let's lead the arts with inclusion at the forefront—because when everyone has a place, the arts can truly thrive.

ABOUT THE AUTHOR

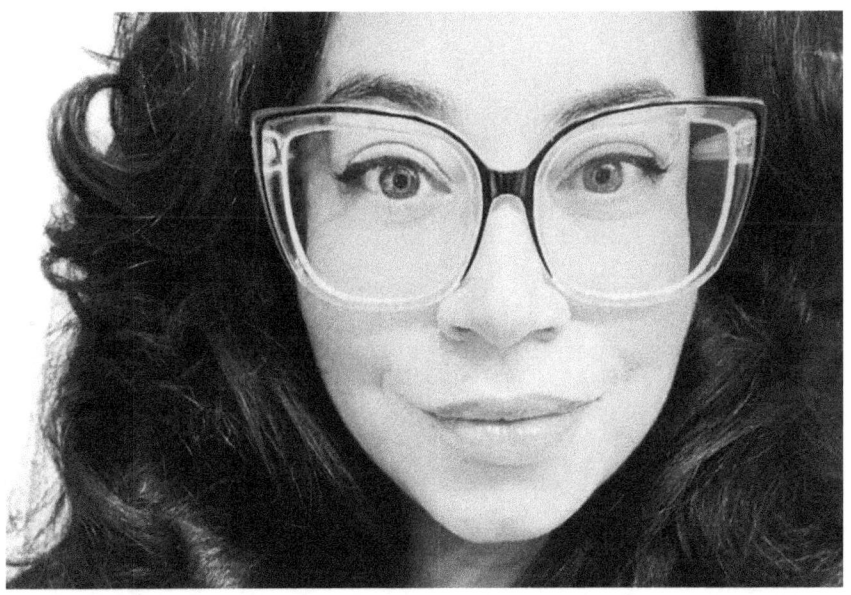

Denise Zubizarreta is a neurodivergent mixed media interdisciplinary artist and Cultural Operations Specialist of Puerto Rican and Cuban descent, with decades of experience in various creative fields. She is currently an arts and culture writer for multiple leading publications that offer curated and critical perspectives on contemporary art, film, television, and culture.

Zubizarreta holds a B.F.A. in Fine Art from Rocky Mountain College of Art + Design, and is completing her Master's in Arts Leadership and Cultural Management (M.A.L.C.M.) at Colorado State University. Her passion for arts and culture drives her to explore and challenge the intersections of post-colonial theory, identity, technology and traditions in her writing and mixed media works.

www.ingramcontent.com/pod-product-compliance
Lightning Source LLC
Chambersburg PA
CBHW070416230526
45471CB00006B/2829